CW01021405

FICTION WRITING TOOLS

FICTION WRITING TOOLS

CREATE VIVID SCENES

SHERRY SOULE

This book or any potion thereof may not be reproduced or used in any manner whatsoever without the express written permission of the publisher or author except for the use of brief quotations in a book review. The scanning, uploading, and distribution of this book via the Internet or via any other means without the permission of the publisher or the author is illegal and punishable by law. Please purchase only authorized electronic editions, and do not participate in or encourage electronic piracy of copyrighted materials. Your support of the author's rights is appreciated.

FICTION WRITING TOOLS

Copyright © 2013 Sherry Soule
All rights reserved.

2nd Edition published 2014

Freelance Fiction Editing
www.fictionwritingtools.blogspot.com

Typesetting services by BOOKOW.COM

For writers at any stage in their career that yearn to take their writing skills to the next level.

Preface

This manual is specifically for fiction writers who want to learn how to create dramatic settings that jump off the page and deeply immerse the reader into the story. Crafting realistic scenes isn't easy, unless you have the tools to create vibrant, believable settings.

This in-depth manual provides essential techniques on world-building, creating realistic locations, and illustrating naturalistic weather, with bonus examples of how to combine the five senses and use deep POV.

This book also explains ways you can include vivid details to any setting that will enhance your writing and how using description can add depth to your narrative.

FICTION NOVELS by SHERRY SOULE

YA Paranormal Romance - Spellbound Series:

BEAUTIFULLY BROKEN (book one)

SHATTERED SILENCE (book two)

MOONLIGHT MAYHEM (book three)

RECKLESS REVENGE (book four)

DESTINY DISRUPTED (book five)

Adult Paranormal Romance novel:

IMMORTAL ECLIPSE

INTRODUCTION

Dear Writer,

I thought I'd share a little bit about myself and why I wanted to write this book on self-editing. First off, I am a bestselling published author, freelance developmental editor (Creativity Coach), and a former acquisitions editor for an indie press, where I edited several award-winning and bestselling novels. Back in 2009, I even owned an online publishing company, so I hope that my insight into the publishing industry and my editing advice helps other writers to find success.

After blogging for many years, I decided to compile some of my most popular blog posts on the creative writing process into this book.

What this book is not?

A lesson on grammar or punctuation *do's* and *don'ts*. I'll be the first to admit that my grammar skills are not the best, but at developmental editing, I think I'm pretty darn good. And I know how to write a realistic scene so vividly that readers can feel, taste, and touch my settings.

And as a professional freelance editor, I wanted to share valuable writing tools that should significantly improve your prose. I also provide examples from published novels to encourage your own creative muse.

There's a ton of great writing and self-editing books and blogs out there, so I hope my small contribution to the craft inspires you!

Happy writing,
Sherry

WRITING DESCRIPTION

This manual offers basic techniques for creating vibrant settings in your novel and how to enhance your scenes by using the five senses. It provides examples for world-building and for crafting realistic characters within more naturalistic locations.

Creating vivid settings isn't easy. Most of my editing clients tend to skip including any background scenery or description to their scenes. But characters need to be anchored to their settings and readers need visual images to envision the world in which you've created.

To help me write tangible settings, I have created a folder (Description Docs) on my computer that is stuffed with files that I can reference with descriptive phrases, words, paragraphs, and scenes. Each file is simply labeled and easy to find. I have files categorized under: "Description – town or city" and "Description – fog – mist – dew" and "Description – bedroom" and so forth. They come in handy as I'm drafting a novel.

To encourage and help *you* write stunning scenes and lush settings, I have included references from my own personal database of descriptive examples.

Why is setting and description important?

The significance of adding description to your scenes and including the five senses into your narrative means that you're using deep POV and constructing vivid, believable settings. This book will help you to create dramatic scenes and show you how to illustrate a distinct and realistic world filled with three-dimensional characters, vivid locations, and naturalistic weather.

The most important writing tools that I provide in this book are:

- How to use description and location to enhance your story
- How to construct effective depictions of characters
- How to skillfully master showing vs. telling
- How to incorporate use of the five senses into your settings

I believe that if you make your settings original, they'll propel your story forward, infuse your fictional world with mood and atmosphere, and add the powerful flavor of emotion that agents/editors demand and readers enjoy.

In this manual, you'll also learn about:

The five senses and how you can use them to arouse the reader's senses of sight, touch, hear, smell, taste, and even feel. How to revise info-dumps and use description to establish a mood that harmonizes with your novel's storyline. How dialogue can be instantly heightened by use of description, and even how to craft unique descriptions of characters, locations, and climate.

Now turn the page and get ready to be inspired!

CHARACTER DESCRIPTION

Like I said, description is tough to write. And so many writers neglect to add character descriptions to the narrative.

How you ever read a book and visualized the main character as a lanky, brown-haired, wimp, only to discover fifty pages into the story that the character was a muscular, tan, blond?

My suggestion is to describe your character as early as possible in your manuscript, but avoid creating a laundry list of attributes by using tedious descriptive words or doing an info-dump to depict a character. It slows the pace and smacks of author intrusion. Now, I know some of you will argue that other published writers do this, but it is still jarring to the reader and in most cases, readers will just skim over it.

A clever writer skillfully tucks the description into the narrative by lacing it through action, conflict, and dialogue. Don't forget to engage all the senses.

As an editor, I find that many writers only describe how things look by *telling*, but you should always strive to <u>show</u> instead by using deep POV. Writers need to make all characters as three-dimensional as possible, so that the reader sees them as real people. Describe what the character(s) look like, how they feel, and how they react to situations and events unfolding around them by lacing it into the scene. The best technique is to present just enough relevant details to help your reader instantly "see" the character.

And I strongly suggest that each time a new character is introduced to the storyline, that the writer provides the reader with a visual illustration. Now, it doesn't have to be a lengthy description of the character, a few key words or action tags can *show* a reader, too. The right blend of description, dialogue, introspection, along with some action can create a strong image for the reader. It will involve them in the story and enhance the atmosphere and mood. Poor descriptions can leave the reader grappling for a visual and feeling disconnected from the characters and the scene. In addition, don't forget to add a few descriptive characteristics, such as the character's clothing, hair, facial expressions, scars, weight, or height. Add action to it to make it more interesting. Keep your writing tight and try to filter out any redundant phrases or words. And add some tension and conflict into every scene!

I have included some examples below to show you what I mean. Each short scene includes most of the five senses and all use deep POV.

Good example from one of my soon-to-be published novels:
Cole stuffed his hands into well-pressed khakis, leaning his large frame against his Lexus. The breeze ruffled his sandy blond hair, and I yearned to brush the strands out of his cerulean eyes. When those generous lips tipped into a cocky grin, I knew I was in big trouble.

End of Example
Now compare the next two examples. The first is a "bad" example of writing description with an info-dump, intrusive dialogue tags, and wordy sentences. This is another humdrum laundry list.

Bad example:
Tad noticed a tall woman wearing a striped skirt with bare legs and heels enter through the front doors of the building. She had green eyes. The woman was clutching the handle of her designer purse very tightly as she examined the lobby. She licked her red lips, and then she frowned. Her fluffy blond hair was styled in a feathery medium-length haircut and the strands rested on top of her slender shoulders. Her ivory shirt wasn't tucked in, and there was some blood on the sleeve. She stared back at the parking lot.

She spotted the security desk and walked across the floor toward Tad. He sat up and tried to straighten his uniform before she made it to the desk.

"May I help you, miss?" he asked with a smile.

She placed her hand on the top of the desktop. She had long red fingernails. Her eyes looked into his, and Tad swallowed loudly.

"Can you please tell me what floor I can find Stanley Martin's office?" she asked coldly.

End of Example

Below is the "better" version of this scene. Learn how to lace in description with dialogue and action. Most of you will be able to tell the difference right away.

Good example:

A tall woman wearing a striped skirt, with the longest, smoothest legs, Tad had ever seen entered the building. Her blue eyes searched the lobby, her hands clutching the handle of her Fendi purse tightly. She licked her red lips, the corners of her mouth tipping downward. She half turned, staring at the parking lot through the sliding glass doors, before muttering a curse. When she pivoted back around, he noticed her silk blouse was partially untucked. A splatter of blood on her ivory cuff.

Spotting the security desk, she glided forward, her flaxen hair styled in a feathery bob that bounced off her slim shoulders. Her stilettos clacking against the marble floor, echoed like a shotgun going off in the quiet room.

Tad sat up, quickly adjusting his wrinkled uniform and straightening his tie. A waft of exotic flowers reached Tad before she did. Tad pressed his lips together and gulped.

Damn, she's even sexier up close.

"May I help you, miss?" He gave her a toothy grin.

She studied him for a long second, one long ruby fingernail tapping the polished surface of the desktop.

"Can you please tell me what floor I can find Stanley Martin's office?"

Her voice dripped like honey. She withdrew a 38. Special from her purse and pointed the gun at him. "And don't make me use this."

This excerpt was taken from my bestselling paranormal romance novel, IMMORTAL ECLIPSE, which I think is a terrific example of how to describe a character:

I blink several times at the dark-haired man standing in the doorway, trying not to stare at his eyes, an intense shade of blue. Damn, he was better looking than most male fashion models I've photographed. Mr. Tall, Dark, and Yummy tilts his head as his eyes lock on mine. Even from a distance, I can tell he'll tower over me, and I'm no midget. He's even dressed similar to the man in the portrait: a soft, white linen shirt —bulging biceps stretching the fabric—under a black vest paired with snug pants and chunky boots. Although, he appears to be only in his late twenties, he looks reserved and intimidating.

Conclusion: no sense of style, but still smoking hot.

A thrilling electric current courses through my body and short-circuits my brain. Matthew didn't mention anyone like *him* living on the property. I don't realize I'm still gawking until he regains his composure and clears his throat.

Stop acting like a drooling idiot and speak to him!

"Hello. I'm, uh, Gerard Blackwell's niece." My face heats. God, that was brilliant. Great first impression. I could really, really use a do-over so I don't come across as an ogling idiot.

One eyebrow arches and his lips curve, but he doesn't truly smile. He just studies me with that flawless, icy gaze.

End of Example

Now describing a first-person narrator is a bit trickier. But not impossible if you have the tools and knowhow.

This next excerpt was taken from, MOONLIGHT MAYHEM (book 3) one of the books in my super popular YA series and it should give you a pretty good idea on how to describe a first-person narrator.

I flicked my gaze to Ariana. She stared out the window, her expression pensive. I reached over and gave her hand a squeeze. Glimpsing my skin next to hers reminded me that Ariana and I were total opposites, like sunny skies versus somber clouds. An optimist compared to a pessimist. And not only in personality, but in looks, too. She had blond ringlets, winter pale skin that had a sparkly glow in direct sunlight, and a curvaceous figure. Me? Well, I'd inherited unusual looking features due to my Sioux lineage on my father's side: an athletic body, high cheekbones, olive complexion, bronze eyes, and thick hair the color of midnight. Yup, she was light to my dark. Even in how we viewed the world.

End of Example

Now compare the following two examples, which should help inspire your creative muse. The first is weak writing, with lots of "telling" and hardly any description.

Bad example:

Sam glanced up from his comic book. A fat man with stringy, dark-brown hair, brown eyes, and a big nose walked into the bookstore. The man was wearing jeans with thick socks and sandals with a faded T-shirt with *Aerosmith* printed across the top. He walked past the bookcases and toward Sam.

"Can I help you?" Sam asked as the man approached.

"Here to pick up my book," he said, loudly.

"Sorry, this week's order hasn't come in yet. Do you wanna give us a call next—"

The man leaned across the counter. "Whaddya mean my book didn't come in yet?" he asked, raucously.

Sam opened his mouth to respond but stopped.

The guy straightened up and tugged down his long shirt with one hand. "Where's my book?" he repeated more calmly.

End of Example

Now this version is written with vivid description and "voice" and deep POV. It shows you how to lace in description with introspection and action. Hopefully, with a bit more *showing*, too. And I tried to include the five senses. Can you see the difference?

Good example:

It was a slow day at the *Book Shark*. Sam Carrington stood at one end of the bookstore in the self-help section, stuffing last week's shipment of books onto the shelves. The bell over the door chimed and Sam glanced up. A waft of car exhaust and brewing coffee entered the room as the door opened.

The customer maneuvered around the bookshelves with a heavy limp. When he caught a glimpse of the man's clothing, Sam's eyebrows rose. It was the middle of summer and the guy had on jeans with socks and leather Birkenstocks. *Crazy.*

Sam hurried past a guy sitting on the floor reading a book and an old lady with blue hair—well, it looked blue—scanning the covers on the romance novels on sale.

Sam walked behind the counter and asked, "Can I help you, sir?"

"Here to pick up my book," the man said.

"Sorry, this week's order hasn't come in yet. Do you wanna give us a call next—"

The stocky man leaned over the glass counter, and glared down at Sam. His dark-brown hair fell into his hazel eyes, and the man pushed the strands aside with a pudgy hand. He lowered his head, his breath soured by stale beer and cigarettes. "Whaddya mean my book didn't come in yet?" His bulbous nose twitched with anger.

Sam's shoulders slumped. *Great. Another pissed off customer. It's not my fault the freaking shipment is always late.*

Before Sam could respond, the man straightened, tugging at the collar of his faded *Aerosmith* T-shirt in an attempt to collect himself. "*Now*. Where's my book on ritual human sacrifices, boy?"

End of Example

Did that example also leaving you wanting to know more?

If it did—than great! I have tried to include some tension and conflict into my examples as well. Conflict should be the driving force behind each scene. Without it, there is no tension, and no way to keep the reader flipping the pages to find out what happens next.

This example is again from my adult published novel, IMMORTAL ECLIPSE and shows both character description and setting, combined with humor.

Compared to the décor in Pauletta's posh office, the furniture is frayed and outdated, with a stack of law books dusting the desk. The room overlooks the Bay Bridge and smells of day-old cigar. *Yuck.* Matthew Rosenberg glances up, surprising me with how much he's aged. His wrinkled skin—probably from all those afternoons spent negotiating cases on the golf course—with teeth that flash yellow when he smiles, and pants drooping beneath a gut that strains his shirt buttons. The years spent in California have added bloat and wrinkles that accentuate his every flaw.

"Nice to see you again, Skylar. It's been a long time." We shake hands, and he gestures toward the seat facing his desk. "I've seen your photos; you've got an extraordinary eye. I'm not much into fashion, but I thought that cover you did for *Glamour* was exceptional."

Apparently, he's the only one.

End of Example

Lacing description with conflict or humor or tension is fiction writing magic!

So I hope these examples improve your fiction writing by showing how a writer can sprinkle description into any scene and throughout the action, dialogue, and introspection.

CLOTHING DESCRIPTION

This chapter will cover clothing descriptions for both male and female characters and how to describe it by using deep POV. I will mainly focus on modern garments in this chapter. So, use this as a database when you need ideas for describing your character's clothing or as a general reference. I admit I enjoy writing description.

Does that mean that I always craft it correctly?

No. Sometimes I do an info-dump, and then I have to go back and figure out a clever way to lace it into the narrative.

Clothing descriptions can be a powerful and effective visual for the reader. It can say a lot about your character's personality without having to "tell" the reader about their likes, dislikes, or background. This is especially helpful if you write in the young adult genre. Most teens like to express themselves and their individuality though fashion.

In this chapter, I have also provided a few examples on writing description, which includes clothing. Below I have placed a reference list of clothing types and fabrics.

CLOTHING STYLES:

- *preppy:* plaid skirts, sweater vests, pearl necklaces
- *punk*: skinny jeans, leather, studs, piercings
- *modest*: covered up, long skirts, sweaters
- *sophisticated*: suits, trousers, pencil skirts, blouses
- *sporty*: sweats, T-shirts, tennis shoes, sneakers, board-shorts
- *trashy*: way too showing

- *edgy*: converse, skinny jeans, black boots, basically some punk but not all punk
- *vintage*: older styles, like an old band on your T-shirt
- *western*: brown leather, blue, browns, and orange: cowboy boots
- *nautical*: blue red and white, bows, and collars
- *summer wear*: sandals, loose sundress, sandals, flats, floppy hats
- *futuristic*: metallic, what you imagine people in the future to wear
- *rocker*: band logos, kind of punk, skinny jeans, leather-studded belts
- *boho-chic*: layered clothing, baggy shirts, big purses, long necklaces, lots of jewelry
- *flirty*: low-cut dress, mini-skirt, stilettos
- *casual:* shorts, pants, tennis shoes, flip-flops, etc.
- *formal*: floor-length gowns, tuxedo, high-heels, wingtip shoes
- *casual chic*: designer jeans, T-shirts, sneakers, khaki pants, capris, and flowing dresses
- *hippie chic*: baggy clothes, peace signs, long skirts, bell-bottoms, tie-dye
- *punk/emo*: skinny jeans; short skirts; flats; converses; graphic T-shirts
- *prep*: ripped jeans; dark wash denim; babydoll blouses; flip-flops; big white sunglasses
- *dressy*: button-down shirts; strappy heels; big bags; vests; shirt dress; straight legged pants
- *hip-hop*: shoes-forces, dunks, high tops; baggy jeans and oversized shirts
- *beach/boho*: big shades; headbands; sundresses; khaki shorts; tank-tops

DESCRIPTIVE FABRICS
Plaid
Tweed

Color block
Ponte knit
Box pleat
Chiffon
Jersey
Crepe
Linen
Silk
Tweed
Velour
leather
suede
Polka dot
embroidered
Floral

Below is an excerpt from one of my novels, SHATTERED SILENCE (book 2) to illustrate how to describe a character's clothing and personality.

He shrugged off a worn leather jacket and draped it over an armchair, displaying a long-sleeved black shirt. The guy was the epitome of hip. With artfully mussed hair, low-slung jeans, motorcycle boots, and model good looks, just a glimpse of Trent Donovan caused female hormones to rage, teenage girls to swoon, and mouths to drool.

End of Example

Please don't do info-dump of characterization. Don't tell the reader that the character is grumpy, or depressed, or bitchy—*show!* Develop your characters through action and dialogue and description. Just remember to always show the reader, don't tell them.

Here is another excerpt taken from my young adult novel, BEAUTI-FULLY BROKEN (book 1) to give you an example on how to describe a first-person character's clothing:

My stomach lurched when I spotted Brittany Witheridge and the dreaded *Trendies* ascending the steps of the school. The Trendies included Brittany's best friend Kayla Bishop, and their other two friends, Heather Keyes and Emily Cast. Brittany had straight hair the color of blackberries, which flowed around her like spun silk brushing her shoulders and highlighting her tan skin. In her slim jeans, she was svelte, with super long legs and minimal curves. She had the same slightly opaque brown eyes and distinct Asian features as her proud Chinese mother. Kayla, tossing her blond locks over her shoulder, hurried on her short, fake-tanned legs to catch up with Brittany's longer strides as they entered the building, joining the throng of urban yuppie students that dominated the school.

I yanked the hood over my head, wishing I'd chosen something else to wear other than frayed jeans, a cropped pink tee that showed off my sparkly bellyring, black hoodie, and my kickass Doc Martens ankle-boots. Not like I was rebelling. I like to think I had my own quirky sense of style.

End of Example

After reading this, what is your impression of these characters? Are they wealthy or underprivileged? Stuck up or nice? Does each girl have a distinct style and what does it say about them? What insight did you gleam by their appearances? Did you imagine their history and background, too?

I assume that you've formed immediate opinions about these teenage girls through this short description, which is what I intended.

This third excerpt is again taken from, IMMORTAL ECLIPSE:

Behind her glass-top desk, Pauletta sits in a sleek black leather chair, which reclines to an almost obscene angle as she crosses her smooth dark brown legs. She's wearing a silk Hermès scarf draped over a gray blouse, matching rayon skirt, and *really* cute Bettye Muller heels. The open blinds allow placid sunlight to highlight the framed fashion magazine covers and commercial advertisements lining the white walls.

End of Example

Don't forget to describe your characters by briefly depicting each new character when introduced, by weaving in clothes, age, hair, eye color, height, weight, visible scars, and even nationality, etc. BUT do it by lacing it into the action and reaction, so it's not a boring list.

This next example much longer and it was taken from my book, RECKLESS REVENGE (book4) in my YA series to demonstrate how you can weave in action, emotion, humor, and intensity.

Suddenly, I got a weird prickly feeling that I was being watched. The little hairs on my neck bristled. I swiveled in my seat, watching my dark hair flip behind me and gasped as a pair of dazzling violet eyes—a sexy *romance novel stare*—locked onto mine. Instantly, a hot flush warmed my skin.

I knew the mystery hunk. At least, I'd seen Stalker Boy before. He was the older guy who had crashed my dad's funeral and verbally assaulted me. And I'd glimpsed him a few other times around town. The question was: what was he doing here now?

Stalker Boy looked about eighteen or nineteen, but not much older. Maybe he was a transfer student repeating a grade. He had his arms crossed and one leg bent at the knee, his booted heel planted on the wall. His shoulder-length black hair made him look like an ancient warrior, and his long bangs fell forward to conceal one eye. When he turned his attention to the teachers standing awkwardly near the podium, I took the opportunity to study him. His skin appeared completely unmarred, with pronounced cheekbones and a strong jawline. He was tall, much taller than me, but I was only 5'6. While I stared at him, only for a moment, the air seemed to glow around his body in warm currents of incandescent sunbeams, almost like an aura.

Stalker Boy glanced my way once more. Damn, he was utterly gorgeous. No one else I'd ever met looked quite like him. My breath hitched. We stared at each other, and a slow smirk spread across his beautiful face.

I couldn't tell if my heart pounded from attraction or fear. Yet, I was also kind of excited to see him again. I let out a sharp breath of surprise. My heart banged once, twice, then advanced into a painful galloping run.

It took a moment before I realized I wasn't scared. No, I was strangely attracted to this guy. Okay, this was getting bizarre even for me. But who could resist a tall, dark hottie with mesmerizing eyes?

Exactly.

End of Example

How did this description of the character make you feel? Did you get a very detailed and vivid image of him? Did you get an inkling of his personality or background? Hopefully, you did!

This chapter and the examples provided should really help you to portray your own characters as real people and turn your scenes into fresh and vivid prose.

HAIR DESCRIPTION

This chapter is for hair description. Don't groan. Now, unless your characters are all bald this list may come in handy.

Powerful character description can add flair and intimacy between your characters and your readers. It will give your readership a strong visual image of what the character looks like. Hair is another form of expression for most people. Especially with teens.

For example, if you're writing a young adult novel, make sure you do some research on current trends and hair colors so readers can relate and identify with your characters.

If your story is about a snobby, affluent family, try adding descriptive words about their flawlessly coiffed hairstyles.

If your novel includes a gang of teenage bullies, include something about their long, greasy manes. You don't have to be cliché, but some stereotyping does help.

I hope this list gives you some creative and original ideas for your own manuscript.

List of hair color:
Highlights (blond, gold, black, red, auburn, etc.)
Arctic blond
Ash Brown
Auburn
Beige White
Black

Blonde
Brunette
Burgundy
Buttered Toast
Butterscotch
Caramel
Chardonnay
Chestnut
Chocolate
Cinnamon
Copper
Coppery Red
Dark
Dirty blonde
Domino
Ebony
Fair
Fiery
Flame Red
Flaxen
Ginger
Golden
Gray
Honey
Honey Blonde
Irish Red
Jet black
Onyx
Pale Blonde
Pale Golden Blonde
Pecan
Raven

Red
Russet
Sable
List of hair types:
Bald patches
Balding
Bleached
Dry
Oily
Fine
Course
Straight
Curly
Wavy
Thin
Thick
Wooly
Greasy
Brittle
Chemically damaged
Dandruff
Frizzy hair
Greasy
Hair loss
List of hairstyles:
Blow dry
Braided
Classic Bob
Crown Braids
Curly
Elegant updo
Short and Spiky

Fringe
Blunt
Bangs
Wavy
Wedding Hair
Ponytail

These next two excerpts were both taken from my novel, MOON-
LIGHT MAYHEM to give you an idea on how to describe a character's
hair:

My ex stood at the counter with his friend and ordered a pizza. His
hair tapered in the back and across both sides, but left heavy on top was
styled into a spiky mess.

End of Example

Every time I caught sight of my reflection and my unevenly cut, shoulder-length black hair, it reminded me of the wickedness that my crazed
mother was capable of doing. Last month, she'd hacked off my long,
straight hair in an attempt to break me. It hadn't worked. She'd done
other things—*awful things*—which I would never understand. Chop-
ping off my hair had only been one of them. And I hated how it looked
now. Taking the scissors, I trimmed the ends so they looked more even
and rested on my shoulders. Much better.

On a rebellious whim, I rummaged in the bathroom drawers until I
located a tube of hair color that I'd bought, but never had the nerve to
use. Time for a change. First bleaching, then tinting a few vibrant pink-
ish-purple streaks took over two hours. Afterward, I rinsed my hair and
peeked in the mirror. The highlights put color in my cheeks and really
emphasized my big brown eyes. I smiled. *Me likey.*

End of Example

Adding descriptions of hair may seem silly to some of you, but if you
write young adult novels, it will add an extra layer of depth and realism
to your storyline. Teens often express themselves through fashion and
hairstyles, so reference this chapter whenever you're stuck on character

description.

This example is from my soon-to-be published romantic, vampire novella, THIRSTY:

He longed to go to her, but remained outside, just below her window. Then he smiled, recalling the first time he'd seen Siobhan in the garden. The first time he'd noticed her unusual eyes. Her irises were a dark violet, which could easily be mistaken for blue and seemed to blend into her pupils. Siobhan's glossy black hair rested on her slender shoulders, and the strands had blue and purple highlights, shiny as a raven's wing. She was dressed in sexy, black clothes—emo style. Her cheeks slightly flushed. Her lips shaped like rose buds, tinted a soft red.

End of Example

Rather than giving readers a long, meticulous description of a character's height, weight, facial features, and clothing, it's best to just show the "personality" of the character. A few well-chosen details will give the reader a clear visualize of your character. Then you just let the readers imagine the rest themselves.

COLOR DESCRIPTION

This chapter will focus on color. With a dash of creativity, it is possible to improve anyone's writing by replacing boring word choices for more imaginative ones.

Effectively written description can present a clear visual for your reader. Use a Thesaurus; it will add color and depth to your work. By creating a vivid image in the reader's mind, they will actually "see" exactly what you're describing. Using color to paint that picture is what a real artist does!

I find as I edit for other writers that the laziest words are produced when describing scenes or characters, and especially color.

Add a Dash of Color to your Scenes!

Color is everywhere, and it's the easiest way to add some creative sizzle to an otherwise bland description. *Be creative.* Use a child's coloring box and check out all the names of the different crayons. Choose the right word, and your reader will have an instant association.

Avoid generic words for colors that give vague descriptions as opposed to specific information and/or describe color. Brown eyes don't capture the reader's imagination as well as *bronze eyes* or *his gaze was the color of bark.* As writers, we have to describe skin tones, hair, eye color, and clothes. Even the look and hues of a room or setting can be enhanced with color descriptors.

Bad examples:

- She wore a red blouse.

- His eyes were brown.
- The sky was blue.
- The old, empty house had peeling white paint.

These examples are bland and not very imaginative. It doesn't really tell the reader anything about the scene. I consider this another form of weak writing. The definition of "weak writing" means *telling* the reader rather than *showing* them.

Good examples:

- Her ruby blouse had a silky sheen and draped her body like a glove.
- His eyes were deep and lustrous—moonlight sparkling on a forest pond under the shade of ancient oaks.
- The sky was a vast sea of blue and puffy white clouds that swept the cobalt sky.

Don't use weak descriptions such as the dog was black or her hair was blond. Introduce depth and texture by saying the Rottweiler was the shade of midnight or her hair was the color of golden sunshine.

This list below can be used to describe eye color, hair, clothing, objects, setting, and even climate.

Basic Color Chart Example:
Cream: yellowish white, light tint of yellow or buff
Lemon: clear, light yellow
Golden: also gold
Wheaten: fawn or pale yellow
Apricot: pinkish yellow or yellowish pink
Mustard: yellowish brown
Biscuit: pale brown
Fawn: light yellowish brown
Fallow: pale yellow, light brown
Beige: very light brown, light gray with brownish tint
Tan: light brown

Buff: yellowish brown of medium to dark tan
Tawny: dark yellowish or dull yellowish brown
Bronze: a metallic brownish color
Sandy: yellowish red
Copper: metallic reddish-brown
Sorrel: light reddish brown
Bay: reddish brown
Rust Red: reddish yellow; reddish brown
Ruby Red: deep red; carmine
Mahogany: reddish brown
Liver: dark reddish brown
Chocolate: dark brown
Dark Brown
Coffee brown
Dun: dull, grayish brown
Light Gray
Mouse: dark brownish gray
Gray: color of ash
Grizzle: gray, devoid of hue
Iron gray: silver-white metallic gray
Slate gray: a dull dark bluish gray
Blue: dark gray
Sable: dark brown, almost black
Black: ebony
Exotic Color Example:
Framboise
Tanager
Tuberose
Yarrow
Jacaranda
Lobelia
Mesclun

Amaryllis
Cyclamen
Azalea
Jonquil
Lacewing
Frangipane
Alyssum
Verbena
Citrine
Saguaro
Reynard
Nankeen
Arugula
Armagnac
Persimmon
Shagreen
Alabaster
Amethyst
Carnelian
Cinnamon
Coral
Crimson
Ebony
Emerald
Fawn
Indigo
Lavender
Lilac
Scarlett
Sienna
Silver
Auburn

Azure
Cobalt
Granite
Gray
Slate
Teal
Topaz
This excerpt was taken from one of my YA novels, RECKLESS RE-
VENGE (book 4) of my serialized novels, featuring a sassy demon-hunt-
ing heroine:
With sluggish, jerking movements, a teenage girl appeared from the
fog. Thick blue veins swelled through her waxed paper skin. The ivory
trim on her ragged cheerleading outfit was yellowed and grimy. Her aura
glimmered like a dying fire. A sickly sweet stench rose from the blond-
haired corpse. She licked her dry, cracked lips.
Zombies. Seriously? Not bad enough I had to battle demons, but now
the walking dead?
End of Example
Are you inspired yet? Good!
The next three excerpts were taken from MOONLIGHT MAYHEM
(book 3) and each describes the setting or characters or weather and sets
the tone for these dramatic scenes:
Outside, the buildings gleamed bleakly beneath filtered light from the
streetlamps and a full moon occupied the painfully dark sky. Splotches
of blood stained the sidewalk. Still wet and running between the cracks
in the pavement, like a river of crimson.
End of Example
The sun resembled a distant gold coin against the pale, cobalt sky. The
graveyard with its endless drab, gray headstones was now empty, void of
life, except for Trent and me. And I liked it that way.
End of Example
A huge raven landed on the chain-link fence that divided the buildings.

The bird's strange eyes eerily fixed on me.

Keeping our gazes cemented on the abnormally large bird, we skirted toward the Jeep. The fearsome raven ruffled its feathers, drenched in moonglow, each black feather edged with cold light. It released a cry of outrage, sounding like the screech of the damned. *Seriously creepy.*

End of Example

This chapter on color should help add spice and vibrant imagery to all of your scenes.

ATMOSPHERE DESCRIPTION

This chapter will focus on how to add a dash of descriptive atmosphere to your scenes. One way to do that is by adding an emotional atmosphere and vivid mood into your settings. I challenge you to try to describe the setting or location through the characters emotions or feelings instead of a descriptive info-dump.

Setting the scene!

Show readers where your characters live, work, and play. To illustrate how you can write awesome description, add the five senses to your narrative, and use deep POV to give you an idea of how to effectively describe a scene and add immediacy to the story.

Show readers your fictional world—a man delivering newspapers or garbage cans lined up by the curb. Let the reader see, hear, and touch your scenes. Too many writers let their characters float around in space. Firmly attach them to your world. This is called world-building. Each new scene needs to establish where the characters are or your readers cannot visualize the setting.

I'm going to include some examples to show you what I mean by adding mood and atmosphere to your scene descriptions.

Example:

The room pulsated with dark energy, as if it were alive, breathing and writhing in pain. Or maybe it was mirroring my own tumbling emotions. Beneath my feet, the hardwood floor grumbled with power like a sleeping beast. The loud furnace was its beating heart.

There is something here. I can sense it.

The supernatural power traveled through the stone floor, seeping past my sneakers and into my skin. That's when I knew that the slumbering evil—the *vampire*—living within the castle had awakened.

Excerpt taken from IMMORTAL ECLIPSE:

Slipping off my boots and socks, I roll up my pants, and walk to the edge of the shore and stand mesmerized by the turbulent ocean. My metallic blue toenails gleam in the sunshine. Dorian is watching me closely, his eyes dark—ravenous. He's biting his lip and his eyes stay on mine. Burning into me. His stare is like a delicious game of sexual torture. My skin warms and blood buzzes in my veins, thrumming loudly in my ears. Heart thumping, I break the intense eye contact, turning away from him to look out at the sea.

In the distance, a sailboat bobbles on the water and seagulls cry like lost children into the surf.

As if angry, the waves crash into the beach, causing me to jump back. Dorian's hungry gaze follows my every move. A few seconds later, another icy wave rolls in and covers my bare feet, my toes sinking into the cold sand. The ocean seems to reflect all the stormy passions raging within me.

End of Example

Notice how closely the character associated her thoughts and feelings with the setting? Did you notice how the atmosphere effected mood and *showed* instead of telling what the characters were thinking and feeling? Could you see where I inserted deep POV into the narrative to enhance the scene? And obviously, all my books are written in deep POV with vivid scenes and realistic settings, if you need more examples.

Example of using the five senses (with extra emphasis on "smell" in deep POV) taken from one of my urban fantasy novels, FALLEN UPWARD:

A shrill, piercing scream violently cut through the cool night air.

Erin ran through the high, rusty gates, her lungs bursting. Faceless stone angels watched her race past. She had to hurry. She darted around headstones and mausoleums. The graveyard reeked of damp earth, rotting roses, and recently cut grass. A late October drizzle dampened her auburn curls and made her shiver.

Suddenly, she tripped, hands flailing out in front of her as she tumbled head first into a freshly dug grave. The plastic Ziploc bag in her hand, slipped from her fingers. She sat up dazed, moist dirt caked to her face and hands. Worms clung to her *Hello Kitty* shirt and she shuddered.

"Ewww!" She brushed the grime from her top.

Grunting, Erin snatched up the baggie she'd dropped, and stuck it between her teeth. She grasped at jutting roots and tried to get a foothold with her sneaker, which sank into the soft earth. Struggling and panting, she finally pulled herself free. Her clothes were saturated with mud, and the pungent odor from the musty, moldering autumn leaves that stuck to her jeans made her stomach turn.

She glanced around. It was after midnight. The cemetery was dank and still. Erin's gaze rested on a mahogany coffin placed next to the open grave. On closer inspection, she realized the coffin had been broken and splintered from within. Something had obviously clawed its way out.

The rancid smell of decaying flesh and dirty hair suggested the creature hadn't ventured too far from its bed. Erin spun around, searching the darkness. Her heart fluttered in her chest like the wings of a bat. The whiff of smoke billowing from the chimneys of the nearby homes gave her little comfort. Especially, when the thick, coppery aroma of blood and embalming fluid hit her nostrils.

Erin glanced up in time to see a pale teenage girl standing near a motionless body. With slow, jerking movements, the dead girl moved towards her. The white trim on her ragged dress was yellowed and drenched in blood.

Erin choked back a scream. *No! No! No!*

The zombie, clearly done with her meal, wiped at her dry, cracked lips with the back of her hand. A sickly sweet stench rose from the blond-haired corpse.

"Aw, crap," Erin muttered, holding up the bag, "Megan, I told you to wait in your coffin until I had a chance to bring you the dog brains." Her gaze rested on the corpse near the treeline and frustration burned her chest. "Sheesh, did ya have to eat the groundskeeper, Mr. Griffin?"

End of Example

Now do you get an idea of how much fun writing description by using atmosphere, the five senses, and deep POV can be? Here's one more.

Example:

The sun crept slowly over the hillside, igniting the dull morning sky. It cast golden beams in every direction over the estate. I stared out the window, the rising sun making the colors more vivid with each passing minute. But as beautiful as the morning was, I knew today would be horrible.

End of Example

This informative chapter on describing a setting or location should inspire you to revise some of your own scenes.

ROOM DESCRIPTION

If you effectively describe a room, then you will set the scene and give your readers a clear image of where your character live and breathe. But don't catalog items or furniture in a room like a boring grocery list. To effectively create a great scene, you need to balance the action of your character with the description of the location.

As you revise, remember that all characters need to be associated to their settings. Whatever place you create for your character, he/she must live within it. It's not enough to describe the location or scenery at the beginning of the novel, and then let the character wander throughout the scenes without any further connection to his/her environment. When a writer accurately describes the iridescent glint of a raven's wing or the flaming burst of color from a sunrise, the writer yanks the reader deeply into the story.

When describing a room don't just catalogue items or furniture like a monotonous list of inventory. To successfully create a great scene, you need to balance the action of your characters with the description of the scene. Describing the setting is important at the beginning of each new scene or chapter to help the reader get a visual of the location.

Bad example:
There was a lamp, body, couch, table and a pumpkin in the living room. Sarah also saw blood on the floor.

Good example:
Cautiously, Sarah tiptoed toward the dusty antique lamp and switched

it on. Muted light illuminated the space. She weaved around the velvet sofa and past an oak end-table, which held an unlit jack-o'-lantern. The stench of death and sulfur assaulted her senses. Sarah backed up slowly into an old clock. Startled, she stumbled to the hardwood floor. Fear darkened her eyes. On the Oriental rug lay a bloody butcher's knife. Sarah's gaze followed the trail of blood over to a lifeless corpse. Then she screamed.

Bad example (boring):

The room looked just like she remembered. Holly was instantly transported back to her adolescence because her old bedroom still contained everything from her childhood.

Good example:

She pushed open the solid oak door and stepped into her childhood bedroom. Light blue striped wallpaper with posters of rock bands covered the walls. A plush azure rug and two overstuffed armchairs flanked a dank fireplace. A queen-sized bed, draped with a sheer curtain dominated the room. The scent of lilacs drifted in the air. Out the single window, the melancholy song of a Blue Jay filled her ears. Holly leaned a hip against the bulky dresser. Her hand lightly trailed the dust coating its smooth surface and she wiped her fingers off on her jeans. Tears spilled from her big brown eyes. Her heart ached with guilt. This was the last place she'd seen her father, before she'd stormed out the front door twenty years ago.

End of Example

Explanations of events are much more dramatic if your characters are directly involved and experiencing them along with the character. Readers may skim long pages of unbroken description' however, if it is slipped in as part of the action, then it is absorbed by the reader almost without being noticed, and enhances the scene. Always try to mix description with dialogue, actions, and the reactions of your characters.

Whenever you describe something, try to see if it can be revised more effectively through character actions, like in the example below.

Good example:

Chase walked warily up to the log cabin and paused beneath a dirty window. Lifting his head and peeking inside, he glimpsed a room filled with dusty old furniture. Everything appeared outdated and worn. Going around to the porch, he jiggled the brass doorknob. The door slowly creaked opened and the stench of mold and neglect hit his nostrils. He sneezed and the sound echoed throughout the lonely room. Oak floors and banisters gleamed dully in the sunshine.

Again, I have provided another much longer excerpt from, IMMOR-TAL ECLIPSE to help you get a clear idea on how to write a descriptive scene using the five senses and written in deep POV, and laced with "voice" and some humor.

As we finish touring the second wing, Mrs. Pratt finally opens a door to the left and switches on the light, illuminating a quaint bedroom. It's richly furnished and decorated in a startling, opulent blue softened by the flowered wallpaper.

The fireplace is flanked by a duo of overstuffed armchairs. Heavy damask curtains tied open with braided tassels cover the bay window that has a cushioned window seat. The huge bed looks soft and warm. With my gaze lingering on the stack of decorative pillows, I almost trip over my luggage and the boxes already placed beside it. My fingers trace the plush velvet comforter; I'll enjoy reading by the fire or snuggled in the bed on cold winter nights. The huge walk-in closet is, hands-down, the best feature of the room.

"This is the Blue Room. It has a private bathroom," she said.

"The Blue Room, huh? Wonder why they call it that?" A giggle erupts. Mrs. Pratt clucks her tongue, so I flatten my lips to stifle the laughter.

I wouldn't ordinarily choose blue, yet the color seems calming, like an antidote to the strange feelings I've been experiencing since arriving at Summerwind.

She moves to the door. "We thought it would be better if you were close to the staff's quarters in this wing. On the other side of the house, otherwise there'd be no one around to hear you scream in the darkness.

At night..." She frowns and looks away.

I stare at her. *As if that doesn't sound ominous.*

The four-poster bed with its fluffy, velvet comforter dominates the room and my thoughts. I plop on it and sigh. "It's charming. And the beautiful antiques—"

"A lot to dust." She grunts, then adds, "Just so you know, the staff is quite proficient, and we've been together a long time. Anyone else could easily get lost in a home this size; however, we understand the layout and the needs. In a secluded location such as this, finding people who'll work at Summerwind can be a challenge."

I move toward the window and drop down on the window seat to stare out. An owl hoots in the darkness and my heart aches. What the hell am I doing here? How could I possibly have thought coming to this isolated mansion was a good idea? I was like the stupid heroine of some Gothic romance novel.

End of Example

As a renowned Creativity Coach, I hope these examples and self-editing tools inspire your own creative muse! Find creative ways to describe your scenes and avoid using filtering words that remove the reader from the experience. My challenge to you is to rewrite a scene in your novel in deep POV and try to use at least two of the five senses. Don't forget to lace in some action and tension.

NEIGHBORHOOD DESCRIPTION

This chapter focuses on how to effectively describe a suburban town, city street, wooded area, or residential neighborhood. The use of the five senses will allow a reader to enter the scene by inducing an emotional response. It works because it creates imagery and tension within the mind.

Also, try to include emotion and character actions to spice up your description and avoid a boring list of details. Incorporating all of the senses in your fiction writing is a great way of making any scene multi-dimensional.

And guess what?

It really doesn't take a lot of extra work, and it's worth it to give your reader a "real" world that they can see, feel, hear, and touch...

Example of a neighborhood:

Amber Street was deserted. The suburban homes seemed strange and silent, as if they might all be vacant inside, like houses in an abandoned ghost town. As though they were void of people, but full of scary watchful things.

The sky overhead was not cerulean but milky and opaque, like a giant sink turned upside down. Andrea felt sure that there were eyes watching her. She hurried down the sidewalk, her sneakers crunching on the crisp autumn leaves. A woman hanging clothes on a line, glanced up as she passed by, and the scent of fresh laundry and fabric softener polluted the air. Andrea smiled, the floral scent brought back memories of her childhood and of her mother's favorite perfume. A delivery truck rumbled down the tree-lined street spewing exhaust and causing her to choke and cough.

Andrea glanced over her shoulder. The woman hanging laundry was gone. Overhead, a raven flew, black against the darkening sky. An omen of death.

She turned and smacked into a tree. The rough bark of the birch chafed the tender flesh of her arm. Rubbing the spot, she quickened her steps until the house came into view. Andrea paused and let out a heavy sigh of relief. Her best friend lived only two streets away from the high school, but the walk felt like it had taken hours. The simple frame house looked like all the others in the neighborhood; except for the shabby porch swing and the flaking yellow paint.

A car slowly turned the corner, and Andrea sprinted toward the house. Tripping on a loose shoelace, she fell forward onto her knees. Shakily, she stood and ran her tongue over her lips, the coppery tang of blood filling her mouth.

The driver hit the gas and the car flew down the street, coming straight at her.

Dashing up the rickety steps, she pounded a fist on the door. "Help me, please!"

End of Example

Now did that scene spark your creative muse? I hope so!

Description of a City Street:

As I walk out of the quiet, air-conditioned comfort of the bookstore, I'm immediately hit by a blast of hot air from the street. I unzip my windbreaker and tie the sleeves around my waist. Tall buildings with their concrete heads in the clouds crowd the business district, and the grumble of trucks and cars passing by resemble a congested river of vehicles rushing toward an unknown destination. I maneuver around a hot dog vendor, wiping his sweaty brow, but bump into office-workers on their lunch break. Smartly dressed men and women hurrying in the direction of a cafe further down the street.

The mixture of onion, garlic, pepper, and other spices create a potent combination that tingles my nose. Holding my breath for a moment, I hurry past the Italian restaurant and cross the street. I've always wondered how the people working inside can stand the odor of garlic. *Ugh.*

At the next corner, I pause, shifting my weight from foot-to-foot while I wait for the signal to blink "walk" before I cross the busy street. The light changes to green and I step off the curb—right into the path of a big, black SUV. My body bounces on the hood, pain ripping through my limbs. Shards of glass from the windshield slash into my skull and torso.

When I woke up hours later in the hospital, my head is bandaged and I'm sporting a white plaster cast on my left leg. The sterile, white room reeks of disinfectant and strong soap.

End of Example

Could you easily imagine that scene above? Could you feel the hot summer day? Visualize the busy city streets? Smell the aroma of spices?

This next excerpt is from the thrilling first book in my YA series, BEAUTIFULLY BROKEN and illustrates the description of a suburban town:

Living on the dismal northern shores of California, Marin County was always foggy and rarely warm. Glimpses of the sun were erratic in Fallen Oaks. A small town crammed with old Victorian houses, dewy forests, and silver skies. Cell phones, email, and high-speed Internet were definitely around, but life moved slower here. And people gossiped far too much and held grudges forever, often for generations. Including the dang ghosts.

Small towns—gotta love them.

To an outsider, the touristy part of town looked picturesque and historically elegant. People often imagined a quaint coastal town with sandy beaches, sunshine, natural beauty, and affluence.

What outsiders didn't visualize was the darker parts.

The lingering gloom. Deep fog that hovered even during the summer months. Chilly winds from the Bay that seeped into your bones, and froze your fingers and toes. Or the surrounding forest, deep and vast, steeped in shadow and clustered with towering Redwoods; large mammoths of green foliage bunched over, bent and stooped, drenching unexplainable darkness across the land. Gloomy skies, scribbled with clouds that hung oppressively low until the penetration of sunlight was noticeably less.

With its overcast skies, a cursed town like Fallen Oaks was the perfect place for vampires. And shadow people. Well, most paranormals would love it here, but witches had settled here first...

End of Example

After reading that excerpt could you picture the town in your mind? Do you get a real sense of the atmosphere and mood?

Example of a derelict neighborhood:

The walk home through the dimly lit streets wasn't enough to drive out the guilt plaguing him. Charlie ambled to the corner, turned, and began walking at a moderate pace. He didn't pause as he rubbed his arms against the icy winds sweeping the neighborhood.

Taking stock of his surroundings, he increased his pace. This shortcut had lead him into a dilapidated part of the city. Storefronts with the occasional apartment above yielded to rundown warehouse-like buildings on both sides of the street with busted-out windows and sagging doors. The sidewalk whittled down to barely a few feet wide and became increasingly trash-littered with every step. The orange sun dipped downward in the distance as darkness edged over the land.

He wondered if this part of the city had become derelict because the businesses had moved out or because the gangs had moved in.

Who knows what lurks behind those broken windows? Or what crouches beyond that half-opened door?

A bout of nausea hit him from the stench of the sewers. One building had a crumbling smokestack that stretched upward, melting into the overcast sky. He hurried past an abandoned car with the driver's door left ajar. The street was eerily quiet. The only sounds were the hushed muffle of his footsteps and the slow dripping of gutters emptying into drainpipes.

A homeless woman pushing a shopping cart shuffled past him. Her eyes narrowed on his face. "You lost, Mister?"

Charlie ignored her and kept walking, hugging himself against the cold.

End of Example

The above example was very detailed and set the mood for the storyline.

Example of an abandoned building:

The desolated Victorian ruin sat regally beyond the wrought-iron fence like a house from an antebellum storybook. The ocher peeling paint had been damaged by harsh winters and the broken windows were dusty and festooned with decaying cobwebs. Rambling roof shingles fell from their high perch and a grove of dead trees surrounded the decaying estate.

End of Example

That last example should've sparked your creativity and imagination. Here's one more.

Example of a wooded area:

The forest, disturbingly magnificent and inviting in daylight, seemed disturbingly horrid and repelling at nightfall. Temperatures in October plummeted quickly when the stars became sparkling specks in a naked dismal sky. I thrashed through the undergrowth to avoid walking in the road. But sharp branches whipped at my face and hands, snagging my leather jacket. Birds screeched their frenzied haranguing overhead like cries of the damned. Footsteps pounded behind me.

Oh, god—he'd found me!

I scrambled over fallen tree trunks, and past the tangled area of broken twigs, but I wasn't quick enough. The knife plunged into my shoulder and I fell to the hard ground in a pool of blood.

End of Example

It is vital to describe where your characters live, work, and play. This chapter should inspire your creative muse and help edit boring scenes into tangible ones that the reader can see, feel and smell.

WEATHER DESCRIPTION

This chapter features tools on how into insert description of the weather into your narrative. And I have included some more awesome examples to give you an idea of how to weave in the time of year or season.

I've read that the climate and the time of year: *season* can and does affect our mood. Don't forget this powerful way to enhance any scene. The right blend of description, dialogue, introspection, climate, and action can create a strong image for the reader. It will involve them in the story and weather can enhance the atmosphere and mood. It adds tension, emotion, and underlying ambiance. Poor descriptions can leave the reader grappling for a visual and feeling disconnected from the characters and the story.

Add the sense of *smell* to any of your outdoor scenes, and use it to make the climate or the season more realistic. And you can also use the type of weather to bring forth strong emotions or reactions in your characters and the weather can play a significant role. For example, a Gothic tale would have a billowy fog, flashes of lightning, and shrieking winds. Cold, damp earthy smells and the scent of wet stone in the castle.

Descriptions of weather are most powerful when it's discernible, aromatic, and tangible. Make your descriptions distinctive and they'll add atmosphere and underlying depth to any scene. For instance, you can describe a hailstorm or a snowfall, an extreme heat wave, or dense twisting fog or a rainbow after a heavy rain.

Use natural elements to illustrate the climate and create atmosphere.

For instance, a funeral can take place on a bright sunny day or a wedding during a freak thunderstorm.

I have added an excerpt from my novel, MOONLIGHT MAYHEM to illustrate what I mean:

Nestled amid hundred-year-old pines, grassy knolls, and manicured walkways, the Silent Hollows Cemetery appeared serene. Birds chirped happily in the trees. Flowers lazed in the warm sunlight. Not an ominous cloud in sight, or heavy mist covering the ground. The languid days of summer had vanished. As had picnics, fireflies, and watching baseball games in the park with my dad. Most of my childhood memories were packed with his love and humor, and the certainty that if he was around even the darkest of storms would eventually pass. And for a while, they always had. A dazzling jet blue sky brimming with dazzling sunshine wasn't the type of day you buried someone you loved.

End of Example

Describe the weather. Is it raining, cloudy, wintry, or sunshiny?

Now, my challenge to you is to find at least three scenes in your manuscript and add a brief description of the weather to each of them.

Examples of adjectives:

Smelly, reeking, fetid, malodorous, rank, putrid, noxious, medicinal, musty pungent, putrid, rancid acrid, antiseptic, bitter, burning, choking, rich, rotten, salty, smoky, sour, spicy, stale, stinky, odor, spoor, stench, reek, tang, pong, forceful, dank

Examples of "smell/scent" adjectives:

Clean, delicious, fragrant, crisp, moist, juicy, breezy, refreshing, unpolluted, fresh, strong, sweet, perfume, fragrance, cologne, aftershave, toilet water, eau de toilette, body spray, aroma, hint, trace, whiff, bouquet, sniff, tinged, pungent, spicy, overpowering, sharp, piquant, heady, pleasant

Where are the characters?

Being an avid reader, I depend on the scene's description to take me away to faraway lands and exciting locations. I love being able to step into someone else's life for a while and see it through their eyes. Like I said, one way to set the scene is to include the weather.

Below is an excerpt from, BEAUTIFULLY BROKEN to give you an idea on how to effectively add weather and the season into any scene:
Thick ground fog swaddled the neighborhood. An early morning hush settled over the town, the drizzling mist softening the streets. I drank in the brisk morning air, welcoming the chill of winter on my flushed cheeks.

This next excerpt was taken from my novel, MOONLIGHT MAYHEM as an example of how to enhance your scene with mood and climate:
A golden sun was swept away by ominous gray clouds. The neighborhood appeared barren; the trees looked like dismembered hands clawing at the ashen sky and the cracked sidewalks deserted. The screeching wind rustled through the autumn trees and dry leaves were tossed and blown like tumbleweeds across the front yard.

End of Example
These next two examples add character reaction to the "weather" scene.

Example:
Nancy stared out the window at the dreary world outside. Faint pitter-patter clatters hit the roof. The wind was whistling as lightning struck the gloomy sky. Winds jerked at the trees, and raindrops left zigzag trails down the foggy glass. A large boom reverberated in distant hillside, and she couldn't help but flinch at the loud rumble of the clap. Pulling a blanket over her shoulders, she hoped that Devon made home okay in the thunderstorm.

Example:
The looming silence was broken when a hiss of wind spun before the gates, and a shadowed figure of a man stepped forward. Staring out the window, Kate jerked back in fright. Without breaking pace, the tall man took long strides toward the front door of the manor, the moon glimmering faintly off his dark hair, thrashing in the wind.

*End of Example
Below is a list of descriptive words taken from my own personal

"scent/smell" database that I've found useful in my own writing for creating stronger scenes, which include the seasons or climate. I hope these help you as much as they help me to revise a scene!

Christmas / Winter
Pine cones, Fresh-Baked Gingerbread, Mulled Wine, Apple Cider, Fig Pudding, Cranberry, Nutmeg, Cinnamon, French Vanilla, Butter, Baked Ham, Woodsmoke, Bayberry Candles, Orange and Cloves, Peppermint, Roasted Chestnuts, Brown Sugar, Gingerbread, Hot Chocolate, Evergreen, Eggnog, Wet Cedar, Wet Woolen Mittens, Bread Rising And Baking, A Pot of Coffee, Frying Bacon, Spruce Needles, Sage And Thyme, Crisp Smell of Fresh Snow.

Springtime
Lilacs In Bloom, Insect Repellent Spray, Suntan Lotion, Corn On The Cob, Watermelon, Cantaloupe, New Hay, Petunias, Charcoal Starter, Seashore, Salty Ocean Breeze, Chlorine, Blueberry Muffin, Gasoline, Campfires, Lavender, Freshly Cut Grass, Fresh Laundry, Cherries, Melon, Ripe Red Strawberries, Cucumber, Shaving Cream, Talc Powder, Sandalwood.

Summer
Honey-Suckle, sea drifting inland on the wind, Orange Ice-Cream Bars, Tangerine, Licorice, Bubble Gum, Lemonade, Ice Tea, Perspiration, Cola – Soda, Sea Salt, Fishy, Seaweed or Algae, Coconut Oil, BBQ Sauce, Bamboo, Fresh Sliced Pineapple, Downy April Fresh Fabric Softener, Fragrant Teak Wood, Clean Scent of Cotton, Powdery Musk, Exhaust Fumes, Juniper Bushes, Freshly Cut Flowers, Honey, Inflatable Plastic.

Halloween / Back to School
Jack-O-Lantern Innards, Candy, Chocolate, Hot Glue, Cornstalks, Damp Leaves, Overturned Earth, Rotting Brown Apples, Roasting Pumpkin Seeds, Chili, Cornbread, Cinnamon, Nutmeg, Tea, Potpourri, Smoking Match, Rain-Soaked Leaves, Distant Fires, Hay, Unpolluted Pure Scent of Rain, Leather, Pencil Lead/Graphite, Dried Corn Kernels Cooking, Wet Dog, Moss, Rotten Wood, Decaying Leaves, Buttery

Popcorn, Cotton Candy.

Thanksgiving / Autumn

Cedar Wood, Bay Rum, Turkey, Scalloped Potatoes, Pecan Pie, Pumpkin Pie, Homemade Rolls, Walnut, Banana Nut Bread, Cranberry Spice, Green and Musky Scent of Bergamot, key, Scalloped Potatoes, Pecan Pie, Pumpkin Pie, Homemade Rolls, Walnut, Banana Nut Bread, Cranberry Spice, Green and Coffee Cake.

Now go through your own manuscript and revise your scenes into dramatic, realistic settings by describing the scents and the climate.

Well, that's it for my advice and examples for writing compelling description. Hope my suggestions and recommendations help you to create vivid and dramatic scenes that yank your reader into the narrative!

REQUEST

If you read this book and enjoy it, please consider posting an honest review on Amazon, Barnes & Noble or goodreads. (Remember that even if you received this book as a gift, as long as you have purchased an Amazon item in the past, you are eligible to leave a review.)

Indie novels would rarely reach the light of day without the dedication of readers willing to post a review. And if time permits, please let me know directly what you thought of the novel. Plus, I love hearing from other writers.

Wishing each and every one you much success on your writing journey!

MORE EDITING TOOLS

Trying to get an agent?
Decided to self-publish?
What to know what makes fantastic dialogue?
What to take your writing to the next level?
Well, these inexpensive books can help!
These other editing books cover many topics such as, dialogue, exposition, point of view, internal-monologue, using deep POV, and other techniques that will help you revise your manuscript and take your writing to the next level!

Fiction Writing Tools: The Plotting Guide
This manual covers how plot influences story structure. How to revise a plot or structure that's veered off course. How to blend character ARC with story ARC, and heighten each scene by building suspense and conflict. Tools and advice for revising common plot problems. How to include character goal, tension, and effect to every chapter. If you want to take your writing to the next level, then this book can help guide you in the right direction.

Fiction Writing Tools: Craft Authentic Dialogue
This manual is specifically for fiction writers who want to learn how to create riveting and compelling dialogue that propels the storyline and reveals character personality. You'll also learn how to weave emotion, description, and action into your dialogue scenes. With a special section on how to avoid the common pitfalls of writing dialogue. All of these helpful

writing tools will make your dialogue sparkle!

Fiction Writing Tools: Craft a Gripping First Chapter

This manual offers basic techniques for creating stronger beginnings and a page-turning "hook" for your fiction novel. It includes guidelines and tools for correcting common first chapter problems and it is filled with helpful examples from published novels. It provides comprehensive tips on revision and practical guidance on self-editing, which every writer needs to revise like an experienced pro.

Fiction Writing Tools: Create Book Blurbs and Query Letters

Writing a query letter that keeps your fiction manuscript out of the slush pile isn't easy, unless you have the tools to create a query letter that rocks! This in-depth manual includes examples of query letters for almost every fiction genre and practical advice on how to craft a strong hook that will have an editor or agent asking for more. Plus, this book covers how to write an enticing book blurb (back jacket copy) that both self-published authors and writers querying agents can use to hook their reader.

These books are now on sale in both print and eBook formats at all major online retailers!

YOUNG ADULT ROMANCE

BEAUTIFULLY BROKEN, the first book in the thrilling Spellbound series by Sherry Soule is now on sale for only $2.99!

They say every town has its secrets, but that doesn't even begin to describe Fallen Oaks. The townsfolk are a superstitious lot and the mystical disappearance of a local teen has everyone murmuring about a centuries old witch's curse.

When Shiloh Trudell takes a summer job at Craven Manor, she discovers a ghost with an agenda. That's where she meets the new town hottie, Trent Donovan, and immediately becomes enchanted by his charms.

Finally, Shiloh's met someone who is supercute and totally into her, but Trent is immersed in the cunning deception that surrounds the mysterious Craven Manor. So much so that he may lose sight of what is truly important to him. And she can't decide whether she wants to shake him or kiss him. Yet neither one of them can deny the immediate, passionate connection growing between them.

But underlying everything is the fear that Trent may be the next victim on a supernatural hit list, and Shiloh is the only person with the power to save him…

With cryptic messages from a pesky wraith, Shiloh must decide how much she's willing to sacrifice to protect the other teenagers in town.

Unfortunately, for Shiloh, not all ghosts want help crossing over. Some want vengeance.

PARANORMAL ROMANCE

Night Owl Romance Novel Top Pick
"…a unique mixture of witchcraft, murder, and heated romance. If you love a jaw-dropping ending that will leave you awed, pick up a copy today..." —*Night Owl Reviews*
IMMORTAL ECLIPSE by Sherry Soule on sale at all major retailers!
As a devoted fashionata and practical New Yorker, Skylar Blackwell doesn't believe in the supernatural—until she inherits Summerwind Mansion. . . .

When her uncle is murdered, and the cops seem uninterested in following up the case, Skylar journeys to California to seek answers. Her search for clues is soon overshadowed by haunting nightmares of a young woman also murdered in the house.

Now the inhabitants of Summerwind are mysteriously dying, and Skylar finds herself in a deadly race against time to expose the killer—before they strike again. Armed with only wit and Pradas, Skylar begins questioning the servants, but the growing list of suspects includes the sexy Dorian, a man desperately trying to forget his tragic past. And a major distraction for Skylar.

Determined to play detective—*instead of the fashion police*—and unravel the dark history of the mansion, Skylar is plunged into an otherworldly mystery that not even she can explain away. As the boundaries between reality and dreams blur, Skylar's greatest challenge is to stay alive long enough to learn the truth.

ABOUT THE AUTHOR

Bestselling author, Sherry Soule is a freelance developmental editor (Creativity Coach) and a former acquisitions editor for an indie publisher (where she edited several award-winning novels), and she was a Creative Writing major in college, and she's also the previous owner of an eBook publishing company.

Sherry mostly writes fiction novels in the paranormal romance genre, which include elements of gripping mystery, enthralling passion, and thrilling suspense.

She specializes in editing mainly: horror, paranormal romance, and romantic suspense in the adult, young adult, and new adult genres, and she hopes that her insight into the creative writing process helps other writers to find success.

Please feel free to contact Sherry for more information on her professional editing and marketing services at: sherry.soule AT att.net

Places you can visit Sherry Soule online
Official Author Blog www.sherrysoule.blogspot.com
Follow on Twitter at @SherrySoule

5630781R00035

Printed in Great Britain
by Amazon.co.uk, Ltd.,
Marston Gate.